This book belongs to

....

Thank you for being our Valued Customer. We would be grateful
If you shared this happy experience on amazon.
This helps us to continue providing great products, and
helps potential buyers to make confident decisions

www.dreamycoloringbook.com

Have a question? Let us know,
support@dreamycoloringbook.com

COLOR TEST PAGE

MELANIE DRAWITCUTE.COM
MARTINEZ

Made in United States
North Haven, CT
18 December 2023

46223658R00057